After the Meltdown

Collected Poetry
by
John Charles Griffin

Snake~Nation~Press
Valdosta, Georgia

Snake Nation Press wishes to thank:
Barbara Passmore & The Price-Campbell Foundation
The Georgia Council for the Arts
Gloria & Wilby Coleman
Lowndes/Valdosta Arts Commission
Dean Poling & *The Valdosta Daily Times*
Blake Ellis
Our Subscribers

Snake Nation Press, the only independent literary press in south Georgia, publishes two *Snake Nation Reviews,* a book of poetry by a single author each year, and a book of fiction by a single author each year. Unsolicited submissions of fiction, essays, art, and poetry are welcome throughout the year but will not be returned unless a stamped, self-addressed envelope is included. We encourage simultaneous submissions.

Subscriptions
Individuals $30
Institutions $40
Foreign $40
Sample Copy $12 (includes shipping)

Published by Snake Nation Press
110 West Force Street
Valdosta, Georgia 31601

ISBN: 978-0-9863589-9-9

AFTER THE MELTDOWN

Poetry & Images
by
John Charles Griffin

Dedicated to the great poet, Seaborn Jones, my mentor and good friend for many years.

Cover Art: Flournoy Holmes
www.flournoyholmes.com

Author Photo Credit: Kirk West
www.kirkwestphotography.com

Production Assistant: Elizabeth Meyer
www.stepwithlizz.com

SPECIAL RECOGNITION:
My deepest gratitude to the following who have nurtured my untamed spirit with inspiration, kinship, and friendship: Brother George and Mary Lou Griffin, Brother David and Judy Griffin, Uncle Harold Griffin, Aunt Sarah Suttles, Uncle Liston Bennett, Brenda Stepp, Mama Louise Hudson, Michael Pierce, The Allman Brothers Band Museum at The Big House, The Wanee Hilton Crew, Wilby Coleman and Family, Judy Puett and Family, Lori Dreizin-Garrett, Kodac Harrison, Don Williams, Linda Lester, Robby Robertson, Alexis Vear, Gilbert Lee, Tommy Talton, Jeff Payne, Jaime Kaplan, Col. Bruce Hampton, Caroline Aiken, Michael Livingston, Lizz Meyer, Randall Bramblett, and Kirk & Kirsten West.

To burst open one's soul, pour out all the ingredients, and take inventory of the contents in the light of raw transparent visibility is a good exercise on the path to discovery, passion, fear, spiritual honesty, ancestry,
tranquility, and peace within.

— J. Griffin 2015

$$C = (O \times I)^2 - A$$

Creativity equals Originality times Inspiration Squared minus Agony.

Reviews

The contents of John Griffin's poems are extremely signifi-
cant & serious. They are written, however, with such an en-
tertaining style, they are as accessible to the reader as they
are deep. Griffin has his own voice, his own rolling rhythmic
content

— Seaborn Jones (1942-2014)

Seaborn Jones was an internationally published poet, nomi-
nated for The Pulitzer Prize for Poetry in 2012. The author of
seven books of poetry, he was a Breadloaf Scholar, and has
been a recipient of the Georgia Author of the Year Award
from the Georgia Council of Authors and Journalists.

John Charles Griffin's poetry rides dangerously close to the
mind's edge but is, surely, rooted in the heart's center.

— Brenda Stepp

Brenda Stepp is a popular Freelance Journalist and Music Crit-
ic who currently does an ongoing interview series for ArtsATL.
Brenda has previously written features and reviews in *Atlan-
ta's Finest Dining* and *The Piedmont Review.*

John Griffin strikes me as a "collard-fed, gourd-painting,
harp-blowing beatnik who manages to be both courtly and
subversive at the same time."

— Candice Dyer

Candice Dyer is an award-winning Writer who's work has ap-
peared in *Atlanta Magazine, Garden & Gun, Men's Journal,*
and *Paste.*

"In his poetry and photographs John Charles Griffin whistles his way through a junkyard of lost souls. Tranquility reigns, but ominous forces stir in the bushes, threatening to jump out and say boo. That tension keeps you both turning the pages and looking over your shoulder."

— Alan Paul, author, *One Way Out: The Inside History of the Allman Brothers Band* (*New York Times* 2014 Best-Seller List)

I know John mainly as a photographer, and in that vein he has an eye for the unusual. His rhymes on the other hand have a certain rhythm to them, that make the words roll over the tongue like a cold beer on a dog day afternoon-refreshing and cool.

— Kodac Harrison
Atlanta Poet and Songwriter

"The love child of Mahatma Gandhi and some Old Testament prophet, John Griffin is half nice guy, half scold. One minute he's rescuing "the lost/art of conversation," the next he's rat-a-tat-tatting all us sinners in "The Blame Game." This sweet, funny, scary book, *After the Meltdown,* will make you squirm, make you want more."

— David Kirby
Poet, columnist, and musicologist Dr. David Kirby is the Robert O. Lawton Distinguished Professor of English at Florida State University.

After The Meltdown

III Cars Money, & Telephones 63

Special Thanks to The Big House Museum, The Otis Redding Big O Foundation, Legendary Grants Lounge, The H&H Restaurant and Gallery West for having preserved and lifted up Macon, Georgia's Amazing Music Legacy.

I

Dirt Road Visionary

Sting Ray Banana Bike

Gumdrop Tree

Raised on a dirt farm
with childhood longings
we started our journey
bent like a bootleg
on southern contraband
colloquial ambition
bible school influence
cypress swamp edges
poisonous reptiles
crawling thru hedges
family farm sedatives
sassafras vapor rub
granny dipping snuff
cooking up a storm
home grown tomatoes
lima beans, turnip greens,
sopping gravy supper time
where daddy drank whiskey
from a coat-pocket bottle
on a John Deere tractor
cotton & tobacco crops
mama at the dime store
green stamp Christmas
buckeyes & gumdrops
dirt road dust pours out
from a pair of old brogans
filling up an hourglass.

Mayfield's Grocery - Box Ankle Road - Forsyth, Georgia

Val-Del Road 1960

A middle-aged man in khakis
ran a dirt road country store
with a gas and grocery sign
cash register making change
loaded pistol under counter
slinging brown paper sacks
transformed open rectangles
where candy & cracker jacks go
where barefooted children
digging popcorn for a prize
learned how to snap fingers
to Hank Williams honky-tonk
hay ride radio in a wooden box
while tobacco-laden pickup trucks
with stick shifts and running boards
armed with gun racks & crop sacks
drove in for Pepsi from an icebox
colder than the North Pole
where chill-bumped arms reached
as wise old farmers told tall tales
reclined in rocking chairs
blowing Lucky Strike smoke rings
crops drenched in pond-water
while drought lingered over
sleds loaded with tobacco
field workers at 100 degrees
where share-croppers in hats
paid sweaty hands on Friday.

Wonder Dog Zydeco - Cat Creek is near Hahira, Georgia

Cat Creek

We drift downstream
trolling motor broken
dodging chain lightning
bailing to stay afloat
beneath a thunderstorm
cold wind blowing
drenched to the core.

Gills hang on a string
full of stump knockers
crickets in a bucket cage
Wild Turkey in a bottle.

Cottonmouths slither
graceful as ballet dancers
closer to the drifting boat
lured by pond worm aroma
hungry to bite what moves.

Distant weather sirens
serenade cypress trees
a wild hog swims towards
fallen trees in a dark swamp
red belly bream jump
over black creek water.

Southern charm runs cool
between stumps and trees
where once upon a time
run low on beer in a cooler
from an old wooden bridge
I caught a transistor radio
while fishing for cat
with chicken guts.

Visionary Artist, Painter Ralph Frank - Columbus, Georgia

Trash Fish Man

He was a trash fish man holding a Bible
sleeping in a shack where water runs deep
with a five-pound cat on a log impaled
slow crucifixion on a rusty nail.

He pulls poison fins with vice grips
a deboning knife on a string
an anglers mean machine
hanging from a water oak tree.

His old swamp dog with ears
nipped & scarred by coyote fangs
howls at the moon and begs
for a taste of chicken bones.

Prehistoric bottom feeders
flopping in a paint bucket
pissed off mud fish on a string
gasp for air on dry land.

A gnashing alligator gar
with it's barracuda frown
bares teeth madder than hell
exiled from drowning.

He was a trash fish man
roasting carp on a stick
cleaning gold capped teeth
with a bone tooth pick.

Abandoned Car near River Road - Jones County

Daytona

Daddy pulled over by
the side of a two lane
highway, took off his
cowhide belt and whipped
me and my two brothers for
screaming in the back seat
while fighting over a dinosaur
from a Sinclair service station
where a man in a uniform
covered with a visor hat
filled the gas tank, checked oil,
and cleaned the windshield
of our Ford Galaxy 500.

Driving past rolling fields
of grapefruit & orange groves
through an alligator crossing
daddy took a detour on a state road
headed towards the Atlantic Ocean.

From Silver Springs
40 East to Ormond Beach
turning south on A1A . . .
Daytona Beach City limits
couldn't arrive too soon.

Counting palm trees in yards,
we prepared our pails & shovels
while dreaming out loud where
smell of salt brought excitement
near boardwalk penny arcades
where signs said "Tan don't burn,
Get a Coppertone Tan."

The Cookie Jar

Mama didn't have enough money
to buy a ceramic pig cookie jar
on Main Street in 1956
at the Hahira Western Auto.

Brother Dave age three
kicked and screamed
"Mama Mama Mama"
while I slept in her arms.

Daddy entered the room
from a local billiard parlor
next door to the feed store
after taking a few drinks . . .
he was cussing up a streak.

"What's wrong with my boy?"
Daddy asked Mama
who replied embarrassed,
"We cain't afford the pig."

The store clerk said,
"I'm so sorry Mr. Griffin
You'll need to come back
another time."

"My boy wants
The God-damned pig
Our credit's good here
We'll pay you on Friday."

As soon as the young woman
at the register figured out
that "No" was not the answer
We left in a Ford with the prize.

Almost sixty years later
Daddy and Mama are gone. . .
the pig sits on my countertop
smiling with rosy cheeks.

Daddy taught me how to cuss
how to reach for the stars . . .
Mama taught me how to love
thru the eyes of a cookie jar.

American Bisque Ceramic Pig - Vintage
1950's

Cricket Songs

Crickets play four songs
on fiddle string wings
in pitch black nights
on cold dark streams.

Mating call that's all
Summer, Spring or Fall
singer of sweetest songs
invited to attend the ball.

Rancid swamp dwellers
arm rubbing charm alarm
predatory allegory in
ancient genetic code.

300 million years of music
echoes across forests
seeking bug-eyed
dance partners.

Bodies plain, striped, or plaid
on land, stream, limb, and lily pad
with a million walleyed frogs
performing symphony in a bog.

Jumping leaf to straw
perked up antenna
fight or take flight,
call of the wild.

Swamp

Fog rolls in
like an old
friend drinking
white lightning
from a Mason jar
spears in hand
hunting bullfrogs
with no worries
about tomorrow
sitting in a used
black Cadillac
shark tail fins
speckled in mud
where snakes crawl
between cypress
tree knees.

Heavy Metal Hubcaps

Hubcap Daddy

Interstate trophies
exiled from revolutions
separated from wheels,
drop out on emergency lanes
and soft shoulders where
gravity takes captives.

RPMs and highway history
vehicular journey-relics
shining souveniers . . .
discovered & taken away
by strangers of salvage to
monkey wrench halo heaven.

Hubcap Daddy's Billboard
on Moreland Avenue says,
"Protected by Dobermans,
Smith and Wesson . . .
We buy scrap iron too."

Decorative dropouts from
automotive Americana,
proudly displayed on
fences, porches, & barns
between stray dogs and
chickens in uncut yards.

Land of Pasaquan - Buena Vista, Georgia

Love Offering

The lay minister intern sits
next to a whore in church
feeling The Holy Spirit
ready to roll across the floor
beneath her fishnet legs
when the Pentecostal preacher
begins to speak in tongues
"Locca mocca walla mahalla"
where faithful jump & shout
smooth talking evangelists
deliver Cadillacs from heaven
eternal life on a rumble seat
promised land prayer cloth
personal debt reduced
back pains extracted
for love offerings.

He wants to know,
"Will she give it
up for Jesus?"

He follows her
to the altar,
falling down
before a cross
on bended knees,
to wrestle with God
on the Road to Canaan,
praying for more wine
and saltine crackers.

Blame Game

Blame the dad and Blame the mom
Blame the drugs the kids are on
Blame the buyer Blame the bought
Blame the sugar Blame the salt.

Blame the matches Blame the fire
Blame the motor Blame the tire
Blame the driver Blame the drink
Blame the thoughts That people think.

Blame the truth Blame the lie
Blame the ears Blame the eyes
Blame the walking Blame the lame
Blame the rope That gotcha tied.

Blame the veggies Blame the meat
Bang the drum & Blame the beat
Blame the heat Blame the steam
Blame the bacon Blame the beans.

Blame the feet Blame the hands
Blame the woman Blame the man
Blame the pots Blame the pans
Blame the players Blame the fans.

Blame the river Blame the flood
Blame the rain Blame the drought
Blame the bottle Blame the cap
Blame the highway Blame the map.

Blame the language Blame the words
Blame the rapper Blame the rap
Blame the pants & Blame the belt
Blame the fiber Blame the felt.

Blame the lotion Blame the tan
Blame the carton Blame the can
Blame the bullet Blame the gun
Blame the moon Blame the sun.

Blame the beauty Blame the beast
Blame the criminal Blame the police
Blame the war & Blame the peace
Blame the most & Blame the least.

Blame the hair Blame the skin
Blame the spinner Blame the spin
Blame the Vodka Blame the Gin
Blame the rooster Blame the hen.

Blame the family Blame the friends
Blame the sinner Blame the sin
Blame the pencil Blame the pen
Blame the beginning Blame The End.

Robby's Bike "The Missing Wheel" - Claystone Farms - Macon. Georgia

Time Forgets

Time moves fast
in an hourglass
actions speak
louder than words
truth speaks more
clear than fiction
thunder speaks
louder than sun

What's been said
is over and done
and you will not
stop to remember
telling secrets
to the wind
while someone
else forgets.

Please enjoy the music while you wait.

Directory Assistance

press 1 if you know your name
press 2 if you are a pet owner
press 3 if you are an American Citizen
press 4 if you are a property owner
press 5 if you trust your neighbors
press 6 if you believe in the power of love
press 7 if you're down on your luck
press 8 if you don't give a flying duck
press 9 if you want to end this call
press 10 if you are a loser
press 11 if you are lonely
press 12 if you are single
press 13 if you are married
press 14 if you are divorced
press 15 if you have memory loss
press 16 if you like elevator music
press 17 if you are madder than hell
all of our operators are currently busy
please enjoy the music while you wait
you have reached a number
that is no longer in service
please try again.

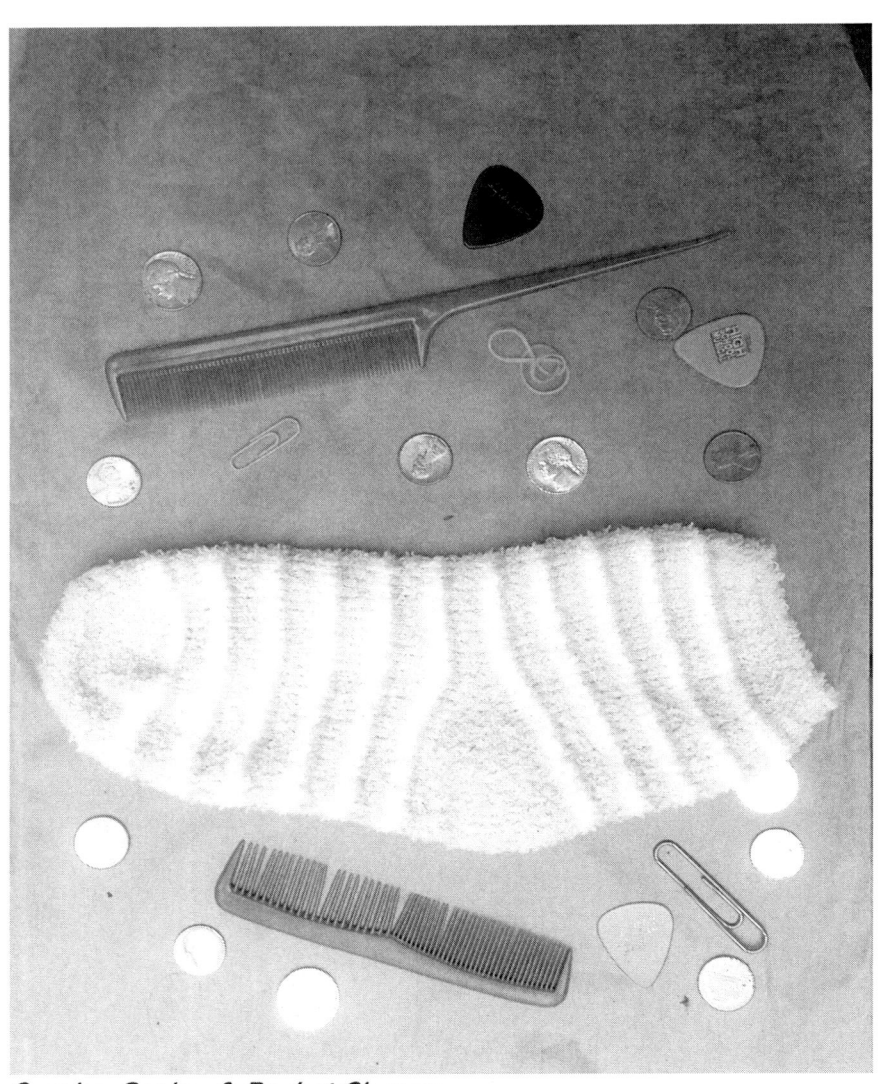

Combs, Socks, & Pocket Change

Combs, Socks, & Pocket Change

What really broke
my fragile heart
with love on rocks
was sudden loss
of combs & socks
things close to feet,
hair, skin, & bones
that disappeared with
penny loafer money
in a washing machine
or dirty clothes basket
leaving me roughshod
forlorn in a rainstorm
umbrella left behind
on a bad hair day
rattling change in pocket
shades of homelessness
leaving a halfway house
feeling like a lost stranger
ancient skull of Golgotha
searching for a Holy place
entranced by Jesus graffiti
baptized by a gully washer
studying wet Bible verse
promises for eternal life
on a book of gopher matches
thoughts from ancient scrolls
while counting holes in soles
roaming through an alley
asking for a spare dollar
in a nickel & dime world.

II

Women
and
Tranquility

Medium Rare

She was a
rare medium
who ordered
her entre'
medium rare.

She was
crazy pretty
and he was
pretty crazy.

She wanted
The main course . . .
he wanted dessert
with an after
dinner drink.

He showed
up early
she was
usually late
stretched out
like a cat
past & future
hands of fate.

He showed
all his cards
while she hid
her secret hand
behind a smile
she was Queen
of flying Hearts
he was Joker
gone wild.

Things fell apart
when they hit
a brick wall
he fell down
she left town
end of story
that was all.

After the Meltdown

Polar bear claws
scratch for a home
icebergs break & fall
after the meltdown.

Happy hour hangover . . .
empire rises, dynasty falls
diplomacy hits brick wall
after the meltdown.

33 revolutions . . .
turntable spins wax
evening news distorts facts
after the meltdown.

Honeymoon in paradise
divorce court in hell
doghouse versus cathouse
after the meltdown.

There's no one left
in the old mill town
just a "Do Not Enter" sign
after the meltdown.

Text message syllables
voices without sound
communication drowned
after the meltdown.

Good versus evil . . .
Superman in dreadlocks
Goldilocks in flip flops
after the meltdown.

33 revolutions . . .
flash dance strobe light
snake bite fist fight
after the meltdown.

Hearts break, earth shakes
tempers flare, souls bare
human spirit seeks repair
after the meltdown.

Shapes of the Broken Ones - Macon, Georgia

Honeymoon

Love is a paper airplane
in the eye of a hurricane
fragile wings fly away
tent revival talk show
thrills pills phone calls
barrel over Niagara Falls
rehab grab in gambling hall
lucky number power ball
happy hour shopping mall
register for free
no strings attached
big screen time share
resort condo giveaway
Baby Boom Honeymoon
Sale of the Century
diamond ring layaway
Victoria's Secret revealed
on wheel of misfortune
book store hangover holocaust
enduring winds of change
Cracker Jack heart attack
road rage in a cat cage
tow trucks in the parking lot
business is booming.

Caribbean Cat - San Juan, Puerto Rico

Love Cat

This love finds me
in a lonely place
feline consequences
climbing walls

I am the lost kitten
speaking Siamese
I am the Cheshire Cat
clawing on bedspreads.

I am the spots
on your party dress
prowling in night air
across the land of your skin

I am a stealthy leopard
running from sharp spears
instinct meanings unclear
paw prints on a scratch post

I am a Bengal tiger
slowed down to a crawl
climbing mountains of love
with teeth and claws

I can feel you
in my whiskers
sleeping on stained glass
speaking in whispers

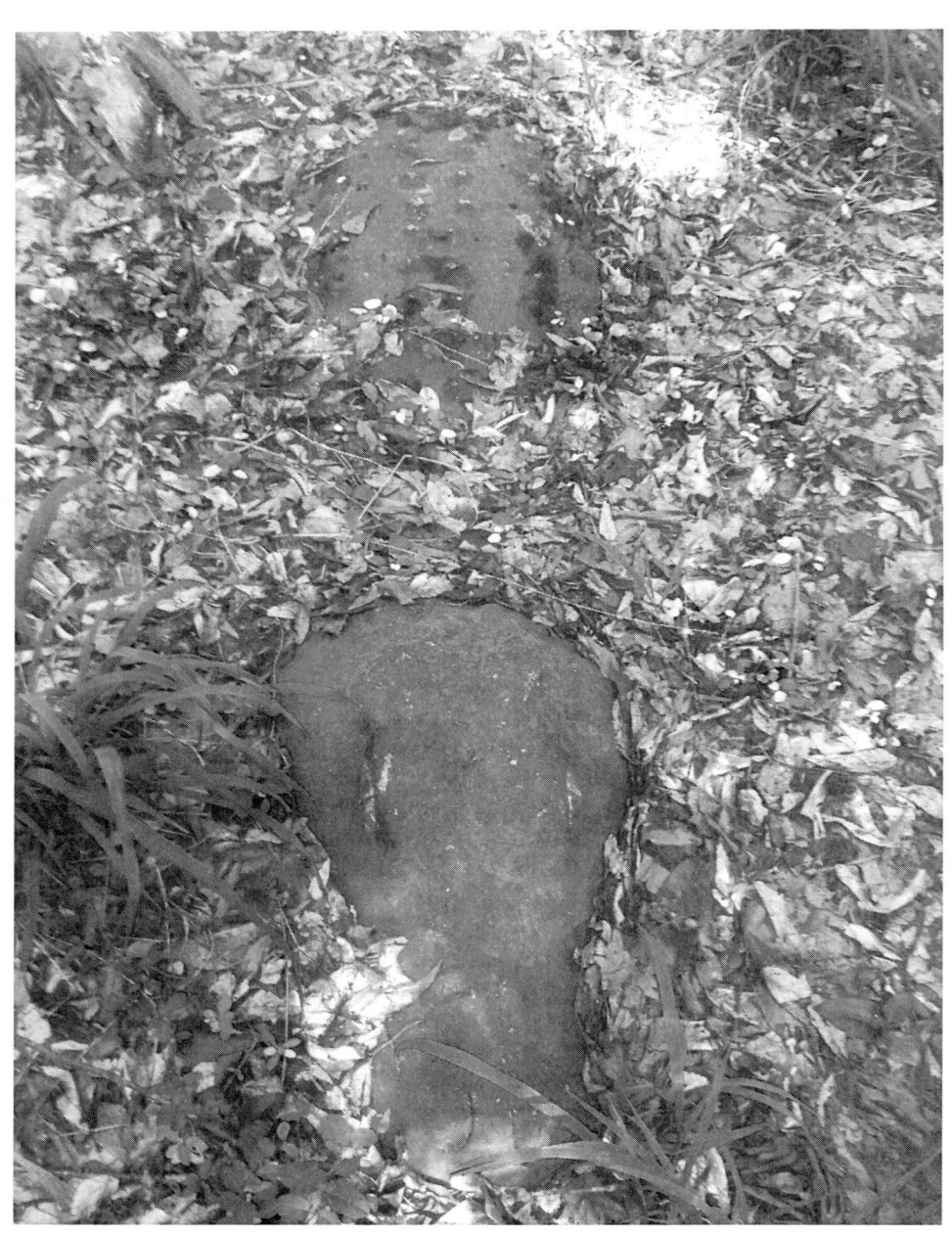

Gator in The Garden - J. Griffin Residence

The Snap

It took time to realize
when emotions unraveled
best to leave the scene
when she snapped.

Without room for debate
pushed to disassociate
always best let it rest
when jousting with fate.

We could talk for hours
what is lost and won
tempered in an instant
proximity on the run.

Ah how unmarked borders
cross backstreets to ambience
where feelings become tried
across mind's invisible fence.

Tested acquiescence
where hearts stumble,
kindred soul distress
within balloon & bubble.

Simplify, sort, & clarify
redefine priorities
of basic wants & needs
read between lines.

The only wrong word
could be anything.

The only right word
        "Silence."

Women & Tranquility

She held jumper cables,
keys to emotional machinery
with it's loose steering wheel,
busted radiator, worn-out brakes,
speedometer malfunction,
leaking oil pan, empty gas tank,
bent bumper,exploding air bags,
blown head gasket, old spark plugs,
loose drive chain, slipping fan belt,
broken shock absorbers, no headlights,
invitations to a junkyard of lost souls
where we drive in reverse to the land
of a thousand dances over a bridge
of childhood dreams across a river
overflowing with love and tears
when night falls strange & gently
bathed in shadowed seas
Nectarous and Tranquility
invisible wave shorelines,
on a blue moon with silver lining.
seen through telescopic lens.

Angel

Did you ever wake up from a bad dream
with the mark of a beast stamped on
your cigarette smoke-stained wrist band
and a Rorschach Blot saying "Admit One ?"

Have you ever awakened dressed in
a Freudian slip with a tattoo on your mind
saying, "Whiskey's Risky, liquor's quicker"
on a hell-bent highway blind ?

Have you ever spent sleepless nights
picking splinters from your heart
cursing hard, cold floors
behind unwelcome doors ?

Have you ever felt danger
in a room full of strangers
or driving without brakes
through a thunderstorm?

Have you ever looked in a mirror
as your own fortune teller
tarot cards cut to the marrow
of your path to the future?

Never wrestle with an angel
She will hug you & unplug you
She will drug you with love
Leave you flat on a rug

Never wrestle with an angel
Never wrestle with . . .
Never wrestle. . .
Never.

Sidney Lanier Bridge - Coastal Georgia

One Bridge

Born in the woods raised wild
educated on school bus rides
life travels dirt road to freeway
to fast lane cars in overdrive.

One bridge stands over the gap
between sinking and swimming
where gratitude steered by attitude
looks over edge rails in silence.

One bridge suspended
high wires of loose cords
drawn tight stretched thin
where travelers lose gravity.

One bridge crosses time and mind
patience transcends guilt sunset
emotions damaged spirit freed
closure unlocks shuttered doors.

Lazeretto Creek Marina - Tybee Island

Low Pressure

The weather in my mind
says partly cloudy women
heart struck by lightning
no romance in forecast.

The weather in my mind
says too hot to handle
cheap wine and candles
no shoe shine for sandals.

The weather in my mind
says write paint create
put away the barometer
of atmospheric fate.

Tough love storms blow in
wash away mud-stained ego
set free, let live,
give up & let go.

Zero to lonely

Tropical depression
hurricane horizon
jet stream wind shear
thunderstorm warning
raindrops on a roof
3-D vision half-blind
parakeet chat in darkness
faint echoes over edges
in dreams beyond time
images on lens and retina
solitary route, turn signals
headlights and brakes
speedometer zero to lonely
primate research project
covered by a rain forest
jungle drums warning
déjà vu on a lost continent
Tarzan on a vine sees Jane
crossing river of no return
a thousand miles crazy
she runs on bare feet
across prehistoric sand
chased by a missing link
on a road atlas of love

Cold Day

Angels of darkness
with burnt wings whisper
go hither and split logs
to start a fire.

That's when questions
came to mind confused
with too much work to do
on a cold day.

My heart grew
unresolved, broken
when a poem flew
out of my mouth
across the room
like a flying bird.
calling your name
trapped in purgatory
pious as a Saint
dreaming of love
without boundaries.

Fiordal Scream

Beer taps
after midnight
whiskey shot
medicine cup
honky tonk
juke box
double breasted
visions
painted ladies
ethereal night
hoochie-coochie
dance muse
filter cigarette
burning lipstick
curves gripped
by fishnets
sex machine
eye shadow
from Oslo
to Moulin Rouge
Van Gogh cuts
off an ear
while Munch
the painter screams
across fiords
beneath red clouds

Insomnia

Diving depths for words of cheer
on wild & lonesome River of Tears

Like a trot line on a rolling stream
heart strings bend to make words sing.

Dropped out over bitter edge
falling miles a broken child.

Dusted off the loose debris
gravitation's wounds set free.

Climbed back up on mountain top
in a rowdy pair of old flip flops.

Woke up from an angry dream
pillow fight with devil steam.

Back to sleep then happened next
visions of woman-casted hex.

Then on a radio without a dial
angels singing brought a smile.

Thoughts of love on burning bed
listening to The Grateful Dead.

Chakra Inertia

He wanted more than
spiritual orgasms
she locked the door
to the candy store
slide rule romance
Darwinian overdrive
supernatural selection
snake charm alarm clock
wires in a time bomb
high fashion passion
nuclear power plant
atomic sonic boom
magnetic resistance
suspended animation
center of gravity
chakra inertia.

III

Cars, Money, and Telephones

The Old Cottonseed Oil Factory - Farmington Depot near Athens, Georgia

Dog Tag

High tide & double wide
Last Supper house trailer
tropic zone cyclone
avalanche & hurricane
Interstate hydroplane
typhoon & tidal wave
earthquake mudslide
burning tire forest fire   ·
train wreck car crash
shady deal karma wheel
machine gun hand grenade
helicopter gun ship.

Welcome to the green zone
poppy seed chicken feed
bubbling crude swine flu
rising from the underground
ISIS crisis sword slices
living in the watered down
looking for the lost & found
covered in a tattered flag
reaching in the body bag
searching for a dog tag
children holding hula hoops
wave to coalition troops.

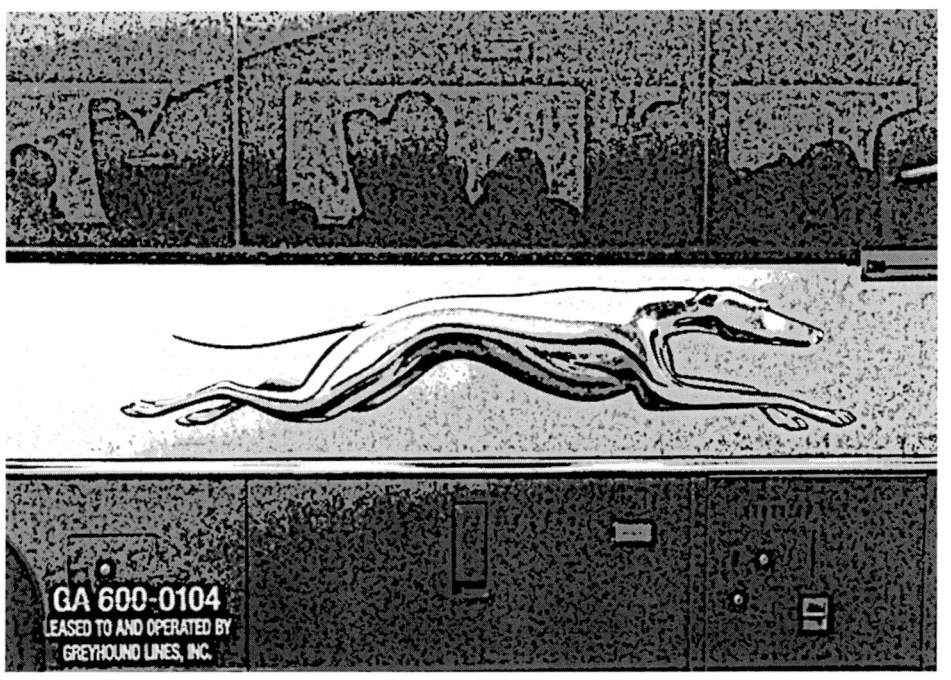

GA 600-0104
LEASED TO AND OPERATED BY
GREYHOUND LINES, INC.

Greyhound

It's two-thirty-six a.m.
driving south on I-75
behind a Greyhound bus
wondering who are the people,
what is the mission they're on
and why they are leaving town
at sixty-eight miles an hour
when rearview blue lights flash
rushing to an accident while
a radio talk show host asks,
"Do aliens sleep with humans?"

My frontal lobe swims back
towards descendants of reptiles
people in transit headed to Florida
some tattooed like branded cattle
walkmans & headphones attached
summoning sounds of ancient jazz
for those willing to join a circus,
giving up the past, selling popcorn
or collecting tickets to a glass house
just a stone's throw from oblivion
longing for lives without pain.

Mogadishu

Primates in business suits
pay the taxi driver for a ride
downtown from The Park View Hotel
leaving cell phones in coat check
at the strobe lit Gold Club
where money removes clothes
to sounds of Metallica,
Donna Summer, & Puff Daddy,
drum beats & primal rhythm,
power & money, sugar & spice.

A tall brunette removes her shirt
and drops her panties on the floor,
cashing in on a ten dollar bill
while sliding the human resources
director's necktie around her waist
where signs say "Look don't touch."

The Corporate V.P. passes a $20
while she blows him a kiss
thinking of her young boy
in nursery school.

She shutters at the thought
while dancing to the beat,
that he will be just another man
who salivates under shadows.

No!—He will become Picasso
Mick Jagger or Johnny Depp . . .
He will sail the seven seas,
Coming back home to Mama
when legs grow weary.

Habib the cab driver
looks at his pocket watch,
remembering the last time
from the back of a school bus
he saw his precious mother
through dust of Mogadishu
standing naked on a plywood box
waving from the refugee camp.

Possum Trot Auction Barn
Tin Roof - Seale, Alabama

Author J. Griffin with Musician Friends Les Dudek & Mike Galloway

Kick Ass

One way street
dead end road
where this poem can
kick your poem's ass

If you ain't got rhyme
or good vibes in time
then go to hell away
because this poem can
kick your poem's ass

No need lock jaw
find a new faux paw
no need for angry lips
step off the battleship

Spilt milk chill pill
thank-you for the guilt trip
fly low drive slow
turn up the stereo

Better cheap hotel than hell
don't mess with my mojo
because this poem can
kick your poem's ass.

Big Bubble at The Wanee Festival - Live Oak, Florida

Silent Treatment

Text message speed of light
haven't heard a human voice
in more than twenty-five years
only letters on a lighted screen
satellite blips on smart phone
evolutionary engineering
vocal chords incarcerated
ambience burning in effigy
voices lost in deaf-mute future
flat lined heart murmurs
at the sound of a beep . . .
While on a trip to New York City
marching through Times Square
scribbling in a roomful of caffeine
an Off Broadway coffee house
to protest distance I send post cards
printing their names & addresses
with (God Forbid!) an ink pen
for very special people who
say they are far too busy
working or cooking, sleeping or
eating, taking a bath or reading or
crossing The River of No Return
while I look across a quiet room
like Valentino in a silent movie
eyes rolling through empty space
trying to recollect the lost
art of cordial conversation.

Ches "The Goatman" McCartney's School Bus - Twiggs County, Georgia

Myopia

Strategic malfunction over
the 45th parallax of lost glasses
near-sighted attention deficit
disorderly conduct stumbling.

Myopia in Utopia
small print incoherent
no seeing eye dog in sight
everything a blur.

Snail's pace in theatre
guided by hand rails
familiar faces unfamiliar
voices in a crowd.

Fallen off the dresser
car keys missing in action
hidden beneath a stack of bills
in order to create a spectacle.

Double-vision astigmatism
seeing two of everything
learning to feel one's way
between merging shadows.

Ophthalmology appointment . . .
pupils dilated with eye drops
chin rests upon a head brace
in an electric chair.

Overhead Lights out, bright flat screen
one eye covered in a dark room
with frame of mind gone blind . . .
identify as many letters as you can.

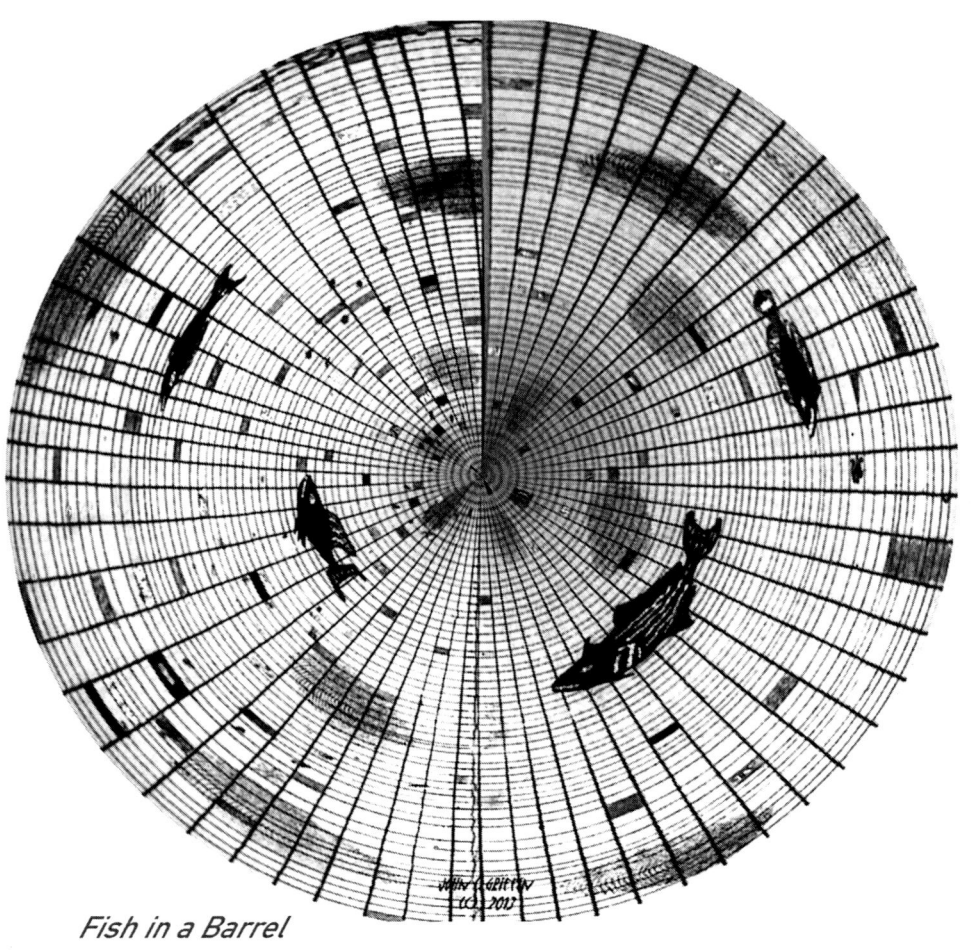

Fish in a Barrel

Feng Shui

Objects and shapes
geometric dimensions
no longer seen on horizon
where meteors cross the sky
only space that lies between
where emptiness takes shape
and nothing becomes all things
reflexes in shadows extended
formed by rays of light beams
covered with sheltered comfort
giving away something every day
so who cannot pronounce feng shui
or comprehend it's simple meaning
should move on to the next page
while soft steps whisper miracles
opening doors for those boxed in
where charity returns in multiples
asking for nothing, silence speaks
more clearly than words

Stilt Walkers - Georgia National Fair - Perry, GA

Crazyville

Some drink whiskey, some take pills
living down yonder in Crazyville.
Some of them argue with looks to kill,
that's how it goes down in Crazyville.

They kick & scream, just can't sit still,
living on the edge in Crazyville.
Midnight freight train over the hill
running on rails in Crazyville.

See how they hide when the chips are down
like a roller coaster ride on a karma wheel
where right & wrong are just another song,
that's the way of living in Crazyville.

Heard all the stories and had my fill,
gonna leave that place called Crazyville.
I just wanna relax, stay home and chill
I'm never going back to Crazyville.

I just wanna relax, stay home and chill,
I'm never going back to Crazyville.

Brosnan Yard Coal Tower - Macon, Georgia

Crime Rhyme

I robbed memory banks,
held up trains of thought
wrote bad poetry and
side-stepped academia.

When I dropped out of sight
I made the 10 most unwanted
non-published list.

Convicted on counts of
missing soap operas
and sentenced to
99 years in poverty,
no cell can hold me
for I shall pick the locks
with pen and ink.

Downtown Atlanta Skyline

Telescope

Land rapers

sit in skyscrapers

natural resources traders

with plans to shoot, cut & burn

dreaming of yachts

on vacations to paradise

baggage loaded limousine

for mistress in designer jeans

adorned in pink mink

luster of pearls

discussing Victoria's Secret

where sugar daddy

leases the rain forest

to a chain saw gang

buys a new Cadillac

smokes imported cigars

sends jobs to China

watches the Dow

hunts wild game

with a telescope gun

from a helicopter

in Saskatchewan.

Billy Joe Shaver at The Hummingbird Tap Room

Honky Tonk

Dedicated to Country Singer Randy Howard (1950-2015)

sad song
honky tonk
whiskey bent
fist fights
whippoorwill
sings blues
across cold
dark nights.

hens in a
chicken coop
crops from
the field
food from
the garden
in a home
cooked meal
for an outlaw ego
with an attitude
crazy as hell
talking trash
actin rude
when the hat
on his head
is a bucket
full of blues
like a time
bomb ticking
with a real
short fuse.

Sax Player Kebbi Williams on Tour with Tedeschi-Trucks Band

Soup Can

Top hat rabbit
reach out grab it
stop rat habits
it's all way gone
Mahatma Gandhi
peace in a blender
health care plan
dinner in a soup can
elevator free fall
saturday night live
guitar fender bender
rhythm in a blender
return to sender
rehab in overdrive
reinvent the wheel
make another deal
forget what you feel
dead line tick tock
ennui in shell shock
go ahead take five
ya' know it's only jive.

Dueling Trees - Little Tybee Island

Global Warming

Oceans have no concessions
sharks devoured the tourists
beach blanket bingo canceled
until further notice.

Bounty hunters scan sand
old men in floppy hats
dog leash on one hand
metal detector on another.

Surf City bones wash out to sea
dolphins flip across horizon
serenaded by fisher birds
beaks dipped in storms wake.

Wings glide full throttle
seeking gifts for a nest
discover message in bottle
pirate map treasure chest.

Hurricane season brings change
loose debris from lost ships
atmospheric pressure rises.
Dreams vanish in amnesia

Old salt sails in lonesome wind
solitude jumps overboard
icebergs fall apart,
sea rises

Avid Bookstore Sidewalk Cafe in Athens, Georgia

Circus World

The bearded lady is ready
to shave and walk away
weight guesser has decided
that carney life is too heavy
fat lady sings the blues
thin man taps a tin can
lion tamer tired of the roar
ready to put down the whip
where glass house mirrors
have seen enough faces
geeks with gold teeth
chew on chicken bones
clowns cry on unicycles
sad faces drip paint
man on flying trapeze
catches falling woman
losing her grip backflip
firm net catches curved hips
palm reader sees the future
monkey on elephant's back
pick pockets pick pockets
gypsies dressed like birds
search for lost feathers

The Old Barn at Shadydale

Assisted Living

No one left to talk to
except Elvis & Jesus
where tired hearts burst,
accordian lungs collapse
back breaks body aches
and memory shuts down,
too blind for television
too deaf for conversation.

Check bounce memory banks
for men & women, rich & poor
tongues tied in knots
by strokes and seizures
sitting in recliners
rooms filled with mirrors
where they stutter & stagger
sedated by prescriptions.

Obsolete faces masquerade
lost & found surround sound.
 "Moon River, wider than a mile
I'm crossing you in style some day."

Time machines remove red carpet
wearing mismatched socks
watching cuckoo clocks
in diapers and pajamas
on walkers & wheelchairs
waiting for birds to sing
trying not to digest
morning medicine cup's
bitter taste of success
where they've worked hard
all of their lives to
earn a place in hell.

Mom & Friends - Magnolia Manor - Bogart, Georgia
Margie Folsom-Griffin (1933-2012) On the right

Mature Audience

Poetry broke the mold
the mold broke the poem
where stubborn habits
jump & run like rabbits
growing old ain't easy
when living on your own

Time kills - no frills - pay bills
numb emotion - metric mathematics
cheap thrills - pills cure ills
unresolved conclusion static
exaggerated discontent lament

Rated Mature, no Parental Guidance
lost in a grocery store aisle
forgetting where you parked.

Tragedy & comedy united
roof leaks, car breaks down
passenger bus leaves town
with cherished friends on board.

Dearly beloved dearly departed
Surreal shapes disappear
taken faraway by angels
past color blind road signs
destination great beyond
inner circle shapes unclear
wardrobe fades out of style.

Personality changes like wind
from recognition to obscurity
while telemarketers target
Social Security insecurity.

Smart Phone Heartbreak

I grow perplexed by
the same old lines of
human misunderstanding
conversation interruptus
ambience in regression
technology heartbreak
reality television
couch potato fallout
kindred soul mitosis
with a mind of its own
that disconnects
mid-sentence.

People repeat themselves
in the dim spotlight of
love's collateral damage
fell asleep & forgot
to call you back . . .
the car broke down
got stuck in traffic
the battery went dead
toilet started leaking
arthritis kicked in.

I grow intrigued
by answering machines
vortex of repetition
token moonlight text
where old wounds open
memories in retrospect
unclear like talking
to a shade tree limb
asking for ripened
fruit to fall.

Every day runs fast-forward
where secret storms brew
state of dramatic urgency
in rush hour traffic jams
don't come over red rover
because the house is a mess
don't touch that dial
unless you have
an emergency.

Mama Louise

Classic Queen of Soul Food
Wisdom & Southern Charm,
Fried Chicken, Collards, Catfish,
Pork Chops, Barbecue Ribs,
Corn Bread, Black-eyed Peas,
Peach Cobbler, Bread Pudding,
Sweet Tea in a Mason Jar.

Matriarch to Rock Stars when
They were hungry & broke,
Hippies, Bankers, Plumbers,
Ditch-Diggers, Movers, Shakers,
Doctors, Mechanics, Carpenters,
Used Car Salesmen, Politicians,
Hospital Floor Moppers, Nurses,
Farmers, and Share Croppers.

Natural Royalty without Ego
Poverty no obstacle to those
Who could not afford the meal
Mama Louise at H&H Restaurant
She is "The Real Deal" indeed
With Kindness, Loving & Sharing
Nurturing and forever caring
Always praying for those in need.

Mama's Great Spirit reminds us
There's Goodness on this Earth
Several Generations can agree
She is a Miracle of Dignity
Savior of Troubled Children
Bringing Faith, Hope, & Charity
Modern Day Wonder Woman
Strength in Times of Disparity.
Thank You so much Mama
A fine example truly a rarity
Still cooking & Looking Good
After All These Years.

Cover Artist

Flournoy Holmes

In his early 20's Flournoy Holmes visually defined the Southern Rock phenomenon of the early 1970's creating popular album covers and art work for bands like the Allman Brothers, Marshall Tucker, Wet Willie, Lynyrd Skynyrd, Charlie Daniels, Outlaws, Sea Level, Hank Williams Jr, Kansas and many others. His mushroom images exploded upon the world music scene and along with the peach have become international icons. He also created works at that time for groups such as Dr. John, Bruce Springsteen, Ted Nugent, Aerosmith, Carol King. His creative, influencial and iconic images are still being used today after 40 years. His work is internationally recognized, in part through the medium of album covers and his paintings are in private and corporate collections, His work has been shown in museums and galleries and has appeared on cds, books, posters and movies. Flournoy is a Grammy Finalist Winner (NARAS, Paul Davis), several time Grammy Nominee and his work is in the Rock & Roll Hall of Fame (Ohio) and his Allman Brothers album "Eat A Peach" was voted "Top 100 Album Covers of All Time" by *Rolling Stone Magazine*. He attended the University of Georgia on a full art scholarship and received a BFA in drawing and painting and then formed Wonder Graphics. He studied art under the painter, James Herbert, interned with Donald Judd (New York City) and studied with painter Mati Klairwein. The jam scene has caught up to his work. Widespread Panic, Sound Tribe Sector 9, Col. Bruce Hampton, Project Z, Jimmy Herring, Endangered Species, Phil and Friends, Count M' Butu, Derek Trucks, The Grateful Dead and Slang have all used his talents. Flournoy epitomizes the creative force, as a multi-disciplined artist and continues to pursue painting, photography, film making and music.

Visit Flournoy at:
FLOURNOYHOLMES.COM

John Charles Griffin

2015

The Poet

John Charles Griffin is a Maconite and 1984 graduate of Valdosta State University with a Bachelor of Arts Degree in Literature. He serves on The Board of Trustees of Macon's Allman Brothers Band Museum at The Big House (www.thebighousemuseum.com) and is a U.S. Navy veteran having served with U.S. Middle East Forces (1975-77) in The Persian Gulf. His photos and poems have been featured in *Silver Valley Voice* and *Velvet Crescendo*. His quotes, photographs and features have appeared in *Gritz* (Now *Kudzu*) *Magazine*, Middle-Georgia's *11th Hour,* and *Georgia Music.* Griffin was born near Hahira, Georgia, when family farms on dirt roads, grocery trucks, and home cooking still existed. Griffin has performed spoken word at Gallery West, Callanwolde Arts Center, Java Monkey Speaks, and New Earth Music Hall.